THE LIGHT OF CHRIST

The Light of Christ

Sermons for the Great Fast

Father Basil Osborne

St Stephen's Press

The Light of Christ

© 1992 Basil Osborne

ISBN 0-9519037-0-5

St Stephen's Press

30 Oxlease
Witney
Oxon OX8 6QX
United Kingdom
Tel & Fax 44.993.772834

Contents

FOREWORD

What a joy and what a privilege to see Father Basil's sermons in print! All those who have heard them already will be able to reflect more deeply on them, and those who have never heard Father Basil speak will discover a new vision of things familiar.

The tone and the language are so simple and so direct that one may, reading them for the first time - and even more hearing them in the context of the Liturgy - take their depth for granted, so transparent they are, addressed from the depths of a personal experience to the hearts and minds of those who are still groping for Words of Life, and challenging us all to live worthily of our calling. They are an uncompromising challenge, but a challenge which is also a warm appeal, encouraging and strengthening our vacillating resolution.

But they also unfold before us depths of theological understanding and experience which we may never have perceived in the familiar narratives, opening to us a new vision, truly human and truly divine. I might quote a number of individual passages in Father Basil's sermons but let me mention two sermons which should be pondered on very specially, that of the Prodigal Son and the sermon preached on the Sunday of Orthodoxy - both casting new light on subjects which we imagine we know so well already. These, as well as many others, have been a revelation to me. I do not doubt that every reader will share my experience.

And a last feature: they are addressed to each of us, yet only in the context of the whole Church. Wesley said that "there is no such thing as a single Christian, as being a Christian means to be a living member of the Body of Christ" (I am quoting the thought from memory and therefore probably incorrectly as far as the words go). These sermons build up each of us singly, yet make us partakers of the Oneness of the Church in an ever renewed manner. They disengage us from an unhealthy dependence on people in authority, by making us aware of having only one Teacher - the Lord Jesus Christ, and simultaneously of being brothers and sisters to one another.

Anthony, Metropolitan of Sourozh

DEDICATION

This dimension of which I have spoken in the Foreword is, no doubt, born of the personal experience of Father Basil. But together with him we should bring our prayerful gratitude to Rachel who was his companion and revealed to him depths of Life which no unmarried man can attain to before he reaches that full communion with God which we call holiness. Her life seemed to many as simple as Father Basil's sermons may appear to be when we first read or hear them, but it shone before all as that "quiet Light" of which we sing at Vespers, and with splendour in her last days and in the glorious victory which radiated in her death.

May this collection of sermons be Father Basil's offering and ours also to her. May she be remembered for ever with awe and gratitude.

Anthony, Metropolitan of Sourozh

THE CYCLE OF GREAT LENT
IN THE ORTHODOX CHURCH

The Pre-Lenten Period

Sunday of the Canaanite Woman

Gospel Reading - Matt. 15:21-28

Sunday of Zacchaeus

Gospel Reading - Luke 19:1-10

Services contained in the Triodion

Sunday of the Publican and the Pharisee

Gospel Reading - Luke 18:10-14

Sunday of the Prodigal Son

Gospel Reading - Luke 15:11-32

Sunday of the Last Judgement (Meatfare)

Gospel Reading - Matt. 25:31-46

Sunday of Forgiveness (Cheesefare)

Gospel Reading - Matt. 6:14-21

Great Lent begins with the Vespers of Forgiveness

The Period of Great Lent

First Sunday   - The Triumph of Orthodoxy

Second Sunday   - St Gregory Palamas

Third Sunday   - The Veneration of the Holy and Life-Giving Cross

Fourth Sunday   - St John Climacus

Fifth Sunday   - St Mary of Egypt

Sixth Sunday   - The Entry of Our Lord into Jerusalem (Palm Sunday)

Holy Pascha (Easter)   - The Resurrection of Our Lord and Saviour Jesus Christ

To Rachel (Anna) Osborne

"Unless a grain of wheat falls into the earth and dies, it remains alone; but if it dies, it bears much fruit."

John 12:24

Quoted at her funeral
by Metropolitan Anthony of Sourozh

9th April 1991-Tuesday of Easter (Bright) Week
on the Orthodox Calendar

ZACCHAEUS SUNDAY

Luke 19:1-10

Each year, as we approach Lent, we hear in church the story of Zacchaeus, and each year we are taught three things by this Gospel narrative: one about humility, one about repentance, and one about the community of the Church.

Zacchaeus "sought to see Jesus, who he was." Like each one of us, to some extent, he had heard of Christ, he had heard of the Lord. But he wanted to know more: he longed to meet him, to see him face to face, to know him personally. And in the circumstances, as he understood them, he couldn't. He couldn't because other people were tall and he was short, he was "little by stature" and could not see Jesus through the crowd that thronged him.

And to overcome his lack of height, his lack of stature, he climbed a tree. As a result, of course, Jesus did see him - and he saw Jesus - but Christ, when He noticed him, didn't immediately commend him for his zeal: but rather, told him to come down, to come down to the ground, if he was going to meet him. Christ told him, in effect, that if he was going to meet him face to face, he would have to be where he was: on the ground.

We, too, have the problems of Zacchaeus; we know we are little of stature, and cannot see. We, too, look around and think that others are much better placed than we are to see Christ. And in our own way each one of us, inwardly, climbs a tree, even if only in our desire, by saying: "If I were different, if I were taller - then I could see."

And to each of us Christ says: "Come down!" "Come down to where *I* am. Leave aside any thought that you must somehow raise yourself up in order to see me. I have come to *you*, to where *you* are. I wish to meet you where you live, and not in some other place. I wish to know you as you are, and that you should know me as I am." In other words, Christ seeks of us truth, truth about ourselves, if we are to know Him who is the Truth. And the truth about ourselves can only bring us to humility, can only bring us up to the "doors of repentance".

To go through these "doors of repentance", however, we must change. And this is the second point at which today's Gospel prepared us for Lent. Because Zacchaeus, when he had come down from his tree, when he had seen Christ face to face and had received Him into his home, realized, perhaps for the first time, that what others said of him was true: he was in fact a sinner. Not, perhaps, in the eyes of the Roman rulers, but before God. And when he saw this, he was given the grace to change. He turned his back on the practices that had made him rich, that had brought him to the top of his profession (he was a "publican in chief", an "arch-publican"). And he took it upon himself to change his ways. "Behold," he says to Christ, "I am going to give half my goods to the poor; and if I have taken anything from anyone by false accusation, I am going to restore it him fourfold." It is only at this point - and not when he first comes through the door - that Christ says to Zacchaeus (and to us): "Today salvation has come to this house." The coming of salvation is marked by change, by repentance, by a turning away from what is old and dead to what is new and has in it the promise of life.

Finally, I would like us all to note that Christ says "to this house". "Today salvation has come to this house". When any one of us repents, when any one of us turns and changes for the better, we are not the only people affected. Those around us, our families, the church community, are touched by God's salvation as well. We do not live alone, in isolation, and what takes place in us affects the lives of all.

So let us prepare for Lent by taking to heart the story of Zacchaeus. Let us remember that Christ seeks to meet us where we are, and that we must do nothing that will get in His way. Let us remember that "truth in the inward parts" will take us only to doors of repentance, and that we must change, inwardly and outwardly if we are to pass through them to knowledge of salvation. And finally, let us remember that what takes place in us and in our lives touches those around us. Through us they, too, can experience God's grace. Amen.

12th February 1989

SUNDAY OF THE PUBLICAN
AND THE PHARISEE

Luke 18:10-14

This Sunday we have begun to hear in Church texts taken from the *Triodion*, the service book which contains all the material which is specially meant to be read or sung during Lent. We began to hear these texts last night. There were not that many of you there, and I feel I ought to take this opportunity to remind you that there is more to being an Orthodox Christian than attending the Liturgy on Sunday morning. The evening services are an important preparation for the celebration the next day. It is in them that much of the teaching of the Church is to be found. It is there that our hearts and minds are best prepared for the participation in the Divine Mysteries.

Yet it is not this that I really wish to speak about this morning, but rather about the Gospel passage which we have just heard: the Parable of the Publican and Pharisee. Along with the Good Samaritan, this is probably the best known of the Lord's parables, and has deeply moulded his followers' perception of the Christian faith. And rightly so. For no other word of Jesus so clearly expresses the reality of a Christian's relationship with his or her God. We are *all* Pharisees who are invited to become Publicans. Does this seem strange? It ought not to. Every one of us starts as a

13

Pharisee, to a greater or lesser degree. And, for a start, let us not be too easy on ourselves. For this is just what it means to be a Pharisee. It means to be easy on oneself. It means to see things in such a way that there is no reason for us to change. It means to say, "I'm alright," when we're not alright. It means to say, "I've done this, and I've done that. Can anyone ask more of me? Haven't I done everything a reasonable person could possibly be asked to do?" (And, of course, we go on to say: "And now it's up to you.")

But this is just what the Pharisee says: "I have done all these things, I have followed the Law. I am righteous in the eyes of God. Indeed I am *not* as other men are. *They* have not done what I have done, and to reach my closeness to God, they must do as I do."

How far this is from the Truth - truth with a capital "T". How far this is from that "truth in the inward parts" that the prophets sought for themselves and for others. Christ says to the Pharisees, as he says to us: "My child, when you have done all that I have commanded you - and more - then say to yourself: 'I am an unprofitable servant: I have done only that which it was my duty to do.'"

You see, the Pharisee has missed one thing. He has failed to grasp that we cannot "pull ourselves up by our bootstraps" and reach God. We cannot draw near

Him by our own efforts. We can only get rid of those things, those patterns of behaviour and attitudes of mind, that prevent *Him* from acting in our lives, from being present to us, and drawing us to Him. And one of the things we do most frequently - and which has a most negative effect upon us - is to think of ourselves as "profitable servants". To say to ourselves: "I have done this and that, and now I'm alright."

Nothing *we* can do will overcome the great gulf that exists between God and sinful man. Only *God* can bridge this gap, can unite us to Himself.

The Liturgy itself is a great teacher in this respect. We assemble for prayer. Each one of us has a specific task, whether this person be bishop, priest, deacon, server, singer, seller of candles and prosfora, or a baptized and chrismated member of Christ's body, called by God to stand in the fellowship of the saints and share, from his or her unique position, in the offering made by all. Each of us does only what we have been told to do by the community as a whole, but by a community which is the Body of Christ, and whose voice, when all is well, is the voice of Christ.

And in the end, when the offering has been made, when we have each, in his or her own way, done our job, then each of us has done nothing at all. The purpose of our gathering, that we should share bodily in the Godhead and divine nature of Christ, has been accomplished by God. We have done - or should have done - all that we have been asked to do. By fulfilling - each and every one of us - his or her particular ministry and service, we have "done our duty" by God and the community. Yet the only appropriate reaction on our part, the only reaction which can reconcile us to God in *Truth* - God's Truth - is to say: "*We* have done nothing; *you*, O Lord, have done it all."

For this reason, it is profoundly un-Orthodox and un-Christian to thank someone for what they have done to help during the Liturgy, though I do it myself from time to time, I know. What is done during the Liturgy is done by God. We are unprofitable servants. To thank an individual participant is to encourage them to think that they have been "profitable servants" - and there are no such in the Church.

So let us begin our journey to Easter, to the Passover of God, by realising that we are Pharisees, Pharisees called to become Publicans by God's grace. If we can all see that we are but "unprofitable servants", then we will have made a start, at least, on that path that leads, through repentance (the door to which is the Publican's prayer: "God, be merciful to me a sinner"), to a willing acceptance of Christ's Cross, and to the joy of His triumph in the Resurrection. Amen.

19th February 1989

This morning I would like to say a few words about an aspect of the Parable of the Publican and the Pharisee, which is perhaps not as prominent in our understanding as it should be. This feature of the parable is bound up with the word "Pharisee" itself, which comes ultimately from a Hebrew word meaning "to separate". The Pharisees were those who separated themselves from others, first from the surrounding Gentile world, so as to be better able to keep the provisions of the Mosaic Law in its entirety, and then even from other members of the Jewish nation who were not as careful about the Law as they were.

So the Pharisee, in today's Gospel, can rightly be set over against the Publican, for a Publican at that time, was a tax-gatherer, an employee of the Roman State, an instrument of its repression, a tool, if you wish, used to help keep the local population under control. To be a publican was a doubtful honour, though no doubt lucrative; but because he worked in close collaboration with the Romans, it was a job which made if difficult to keep the Law. The Publican, then, was in some ways the opposite of the Pharisee in that he did not, for the sake of his religion, separate himself from the surrounding world to live in the purity, both moral and ritual, of isolation.

The world from which the Pharisee separated himself was, in our terms, the secular world, a world in which the insights and understandings of traditional life and faith were being sold at a discount: where they no longer seemed to be worth very much. And this was precisely the world in which the Publican had immersed hiself, compromising himself in terms of the Law, turning aside from the faith of his fathers, from the legislation divinely revealed to Moses.

How, then, can the Publican be the "hero" of this Parable? How can he go down from the temple justified, rather that the Pharisee? The answer is given in a verse which we did not hear this morning, but is used in St Luke's Gospel to introduce Christ's words: "And the Lord spake this parable unto certain which trusted in themselves that they were righteous, and despised others." Those who relied on, who were confident in their own ability to keep the Law, and who felt that, having kept the Law, they were righteous in God's eyes.

But the whole thrust of Christ's teaching is in the other direction. In the preceding chapter of St Luke He asks, "Does the master thank the servant because he did the things that were commanded him?" No. "So likewise you, when you have done all those things which were commanded you, say, 'We are unprofitable servants: we have done that which was our duty to do.'"

The feeling of righteousness, Christ says, which comes from fulfilling the Law, is not pleasing in God's eyes. This is true of both the Old Testament Law, and the New, of the Law of Moses and of the Law of Christ. We can see this clearly in the Parable of the Sheep and the Goats, where it is very important that the righteous are unaware that they have fed and clothed Christ when they fed and clothed the poor. Because they were unaware, they were unable to compliment themselves on what they had done, and thus their amazement is an important element in their being placed by Christ on the right hand of God.

How far we are from them, how far we are from the Publican. The former were righteous in God's eyes and did not know it; the latter was unrighteous, and was completely aware that he had done nothing to justify fellowship with God. What is common to both cases is that none of them "trusted in himself", the former when they might have done so, the latter because he saw quite rightly that he couldn't.

Let us learn, then, from today's Parable, not to have confidence in what we ourselves can do. Salvation comes to those who can stand as sinners before God. And let us learn also that the path of the Pharisee, whereby he separated himself from the surrounding world, from that hellenized, "secularized" world - in the interests of his own salvation, is not what Christ has in mind when He says, "Follow me." There are many temptations along the path of the Pharisee, not the least of which is that we may easily say, when we have finally separated ourselves from the surrounding "secular" world, "I thank you, God, that I am not as other men."

May we all come to realize with increased clarity that Christ came to save all men. May our faith in God's strength and our love grow to such a point that we no longer need to cut ourselves off from anyone. Amen.

8th February 1987

SUNDAY OF THE PRODIGAL SON

Luke 15:11-32

Today's Gospel reading, the parable of the Prodigal Son, greets us every year in this period of preparation for Lent. It is a marvellous parable and is able, like all parables, to focus our attention upon both what is little and what is great, what is near at hand and what is far away, on what concerns ourselves and what concerns the whole of creation.

This morning I wish to say a few words about the more far-reaching implications of the parable of the Prodigal Son. About what it says about the Trinity and about the final destiny of man. Because what we have in this parable, if we look at it closely, is nothing less than an account of the creation of man and a description of his final destiny, compressed into a single story.

Let us begin with the father. He is the central figure in the narration and determines the course of the whole story. As father of two sons, he appears as the author, the creator of life. He is also a man of power; the wealth of the family, its material possessions are entirely at his disposal, they are all in his hands. And yet, at the very beginning of the parable, we are shown, in his reply to the younger son's demands, one of the most generous, self-sacrificing acts that we come across in the Gospels. In fact it bears comparison only to the Crucifixion and is kenotic, i.e. self-emptying in the same way. Because the father accepts to be treated by his son as if he were dead. He does not die, but in the inner structure of their relationship it is as if he had died, as if he were dead.

And what does this mean for the son? It means that he has been given complete and perfect freedom. The freedom to act as if his father no longer existed, the freedom to treat him as if he were nothing. And this was what God did for man at his creation. He left him free to treat Him as if He did not exist, as if He, the Creator, were dead, even to kill Him if he wished to.

In effect, the creation of man contains the Cross. As a kenotic act, as an act of self-emptying, the creation of man by God contains the death of God on the Cross. And this is why St John can speak in Revelation about "the Lamb slain from the foundation of world". There is a sense in which the Crucifixion adds nothing to Creation.

In this way, then, the Parable of the Prodigal Son points back to the beginning of all things and gives us an insight into the kind of God who created the world. But at the same time it looks forward to the end of all things and shows us the purpose of this same Creation. It shows us why God created man.

The goal of all action in the parable, the focus of its

meaning does not actually lie in the return of the son. It lies beyond this, in the feast which the father provides for him when he finally does come home. This feast, for which somehow a fatted calf is conveniently at hand, cannot be separated from the father's granting his son his portion of the inheritance. Nor can it be separated from God's creation of man. It is contained in both of them in the form of hope. In the form of longing. In the longing for the son's return, in the hope that man will, in his freedom, return to share his life again with the Creator.

And it is here that I see the trinitarian character of the parable. Because the son is not invited to celebrate his return by dining with the father alone. The older brother is also to have a part in the feast. And the fact that in the parable the older brother cannot bring himself to rejoice, only serves to emphasize the inter-personal, trinitarian character of the feast itself. The Trinity is the model through which the behaviour of the older son is to be understood and against which it is to be judged.

Here, too, we return to the beginning. The creation of the world by the Father somehow contains in it the Crucifixion of the Son and His rising from the dead in the power of the Holy Spirit. But then the hope of the Father for the ultimate fulfilment of creation in the free return of the men and women whom He has created is a hope, a longing that man will come one day not only to share His company, not only feast with Him, but will come to share the joy and the life which He Himself shares with the Son and the Holy Spirit.

And this is the final point I want to make. Today's parable is about repentance. On the surface it might seem that this concerns only the prodigal himself and his father; and that the repentance itself involves only the son. But if we use the parable to understand the greater issues of the creation and final destiny of man, we can see in it marked trinitarian implications. And the most important of these, at this moment of the Church's year, lies in what it says about repentance. Because it says that the ultimate goal of repentance is not individual salvation, not even reconciliation with someone else, but life in community, life in the model of the Holy Trinity, a life in which we do not hold on to what we have, but share it.

May God grant us all the grace of repentance, that turning away from self-centredness to life in communion with the Holy Trinity: Father, Son and Holy Spirit. A life which is open to others, as the persons of the Godhead are open to each other and to us. Amen.

14th February 1982

SUNDAY OF THE LAST JUDGEMENT

Matt. 25:31-46

Each year as Lent draws near we hear this Gospel reading, the Parable of the Sheep and the Goats. And each year it comes like a knife to cut to the heart of our complacency, our self-satisfaction, our conviction that somehow we are alright with God. There is no Gospel reading better suited for conveying to us this vital message: we are not yet Christians; we are not yet followers of Christ.

And how does this Gospel do this? By placing us at the end of time, by showing us the moment when Christ will come again, "to judge both the living and the dead", as we say in the Creed, by introducing to us the way God looks at us and at the world.

Last week I spoke about how God emptied Himself in order to create, about how He had to create a space where He was not, in order to create us and the world from nothing. About how this personal kenosis, this original self-emptying, contained in itself the coming Crucifixion, the Lamb slain from the foundation of the world, from the very beginning of time.

Today's Gospel takes us to the end of time, to the moment of the fulfilment of all things, when God will be all in all. It is at that moment that final judgement will take place. And what is marvellous is that the end corresponds to the beginning. The judgment of man by God is bound up inextricably with man's creation by God: the one is a reflection, indeed an icon of the other. God created us - and re-created us in Christ - by emptying Himself. Because the kenosis of God in creation and in Christ is a gift: God both gives being to man initially, drawing being out of nothingness, and restores man to true existence by giving Himself in the form of His Son, both in the Incarnation and in the mysteries of the Church.

The final judgment takes place against the background of that gift: in today's Gospel Christ tells the righteous what they have done to deserve to stand on His right hand. They have given: they have given food; they have given drink; they have given a place in their home; they have given clothing; they have given comfort; they have given time. In doing this they have done no more than given what they have received - what they have received from God.

The judgment of men, then, takes place in the light of the Creation: through the Parable of the Sheep and the Goats we gain an insight into what took place at the foundation of the world.

But it is not just the question of giving that links the beginning and the end of all things. God's gift of being in creation takes place against the background of the void, in the face of nothingness, in an absence of life and of being. It takes place where there is no hope of any gift in return. And this is the image against which we shall all be judged. Not whether we have given clothes to those who have clothes already, or food to those who already have plenty to eat, or have visited those who will then return our visit; have given shelter to those who already have a place to live and can offer us shelter in return. This is not what God did in creation and it is not what He is asking of us now. No. At the Last Judgement God will only be interested in what we gave when there was no prospect of return. When our gift was a pure gift, into the emptiness of hunger, thirst and need.

All this may seem clear enough. But there is another aspect of this question which I think it may be more difficult to accept and understand. To whom did the Father send His Son? To those who were in possession of God? To those whose lives were already filled with God, with concern for the Law and for righteousness? To those who were already concerned for the niceties of their relationship with God? No. He sent His Son to those places where God was not, to peoples for whom the name of God was nothing. He sent Him into emptiness, into drabness, into the void. He sent Him not to those who wanted God, but to those whom God wanted. He sent Him not where He could expect a generous response, where He would receive approval, where people would automatically say: "Yes, this is what we wanted to hear." He sent Him where He could expect to receive nothing. He sent Him where God was not. And it is against this image also that we shall be judged on the Last Day.

How often do we take the Gospel, the message of Christ, to places where Christ is not? How often do we speak into the void, into the nothingness, into the godlessness of the world in which we live? How often do we preach where there are no grounds for expecting a response? What we do - and I am talking about myself - is preach to the converted, to those who want God, and not to those whom God wants. And because of this, because we offer the riches of the Gospel to those who are already quite well fed; because we offer this cup of salvation to those who are already drinking from the cup; because we offer a home and fellowship to those who already belong, quite consciously, to the family of God - it is because of this that we run the risk of finding ourselves placed on Christ's left side on the Last Day.

If we want to be true to the Incarnation, if we are to be true to God's love for man and for His world, we must reach out into the void, into the coldness which is the absence of God, and bring the Gospel there, far beyond the confines of our own communities. We Orthodox in this country have not yet even begun to do this. And until we do so, we stand under the judgment of today's Parable; until we do so we have not even begun to give human flesh to the love of God. Amen.

21st February 1982

In the Gospels there are two great parables through which Christ speaks to us about what things will be like in the last days and after death - the Parable of Lazarus, who ate the crumbs which fell from the Rich Man's table, and today's Parable of the Sheep and the Goats. In both these passages we get a picture of a great divide that exists between heaven and hell, between those who enjoy God's blesing and those in torment, between those whom Christ calls "the blessed of the Father" and those who are condemned to the "everlasting fire prepared for the devil and his angels". In the words of Abraham from the story of Lazarus the beggar, "between us and you" - between those in heaven and those in hell - "there is a great gulf fixed, so that they which would pass from hence to you cannot; neither can they pass to us who would come from thence."

In the Gospels we are told of this as if it were something that would apply to us after death. But what I want to suggest this morning is that, just as the reality of the

Messianic banquet of the just is present in this world, before the end, in the divine Liturgy of the Church, and just as the Second Coming is experienced in the Eucharistic Mystery as a present reality, so these two conditions of man, blessedness and eternal torment, are experienced in this world now, and that we all, to some degree at least, know what they are. In fact, it is only because of this that these parables can have any meaning for us at all.

But whereas at the end of time, a "great gulf" will separate these two conditions, in this world, where the glory of God and the triumph of God are still hidden, they exist in the closest conjunction with each other. Solzhenitsyn has said, in a memorable phrase, that "the dividing line between good and evil passes through the heart of every man." In this world the same can be said of heaven and hell: they exist outside of us in the closest conjunction, they exist within us, intertwined, as well.

In this world hell is not something far away from the righteous, nor is heaven something far away from the sinner. These realities of the last days penetrate our world and can be found in the heart of each and every one of us. In fact, if we but saw these things clearly, we would know that we stand, at every moment, on the border line between them, in a position to move towards one or the other.

In one of the earliest examples of Christian literature outside the New Testament, in the so-called "Teaching of the Twelve Apostles", the experience of the Christian is likened to that of a traveller who comes upon a fork in the road: he must choose, and the choice is between good and evil, between life and death. But we all stand at the crossroads, all the time, and are constantly choosing, sometimes in awareness of what we are doing, sometimes not.

The same can be said of today's Parable of the Sheep and the Goats: the decision we make as regards feeding the hungry, clothing the naked, tending the sick and bringing help to those in prison, if we generalize our understanding of them, as we must, can be seen to take place at every moment of our lives. So not only are heaven and hell present realities, available here for us to experience in anticipation of the last days, but the choices that lead us one way or the other are being made all the time.

At every moment of our lives we stand at the crossroads, poised to move one way or the other. And the purpose of Great Lent, the purpose of all ascetic endeavour, is to free us to make decisions. Behind all our vocabulary of repentance, of change of mind, change of heart, lies the fundamental Old Testament, Hebrew notion of "turning". To repent is to turn. And since we can never stand still, to "turn" means to move off in a new direction.

Let us remember, then, as we draw near to Lent, that even if a great gulf separates Lazarus and the Rich Man in the next world, in this world we stand at the meeting point between life and death, between the kingdom prepared "from the foundation of the world" and the "everlasting fire"; that we stand always at the crossroads, and that to turn even slightly, to change the direction of our lives, can bring us to knowledge of eternal life. Amen.

14th February 1988

FORGIVENESS (CHEESEFARE) SUNDAY

John 15:15

Last night's Vigil Service was full of references to the expulsion of Adam and Eve from Paradise: the lament of mankind as we stand on the outside looking in, exiled from our true home, which can be defined as a world in which man and God live together as friends: not as equals, but as friends, with all the closeness and intimacy that friendship implies. It is this that gives poignancy to Jesus' words to his disciples: "Henceforth I call you friends; for all things that I have of the Father I have made known unto you." The disciples have been drawn into the circle of Christ's friendship, to share his life, to receive from Him what he himself had received from his Father.

It is the intimacy of friendship that speaks also in the way that John the Baptist calls himself "the friend of the bridegroom", the friend who accompanies the bridegroom into the bridal chamber - and then withdraws, that the groom may be alone with the bride. It is this closeness that speaks to us in the words of Christ, "Our friend Lazarus sleepeth," which then become "Lazarus is dead." Words which somehow reveal the inner nature of Christian community. It is also the closeness and the intimacy of friendship that give depth and at the same time cutting power to the words which Christ spoke to Judas in the Garden of Gethsemane after he had betrayed Him with a kiss: "Friend, wherefore art thou come?" In the word "friend" addressed to Judas can be found all the sorrow and pain of man since his self-willed exile from Paradise. Like Adam, Judas had received the gift of intimacy with God, but had turned from it in his pride to worshipping idols of his own making. At the very threshold of the Resurrection, at the very threshold of eternal life, man, in his freedom, is still capable of turning away from God.

The whole of Lent is about our turning back to God, about our restoration to friendship with our Creator through obedience and repentance; through reversing, with the help of God's grace, the process which led to our estrangement in the first place. Today's Gospel passage dwells on three aspects of this return: first, the need to forgive others if we wish to receive the forgiveness of God. This requirement is presented here in a categorical way: "If ye forgive not men their trespasses, neither will your Father forgive your trespasses." We are presented with a law of the spirit, quite as inexorable as any law that operates in the material world. And we are invited to come to terms with it almost as if it were some Newtonian law of motion.

Then, secondly, we are told to avoid hypocrisy, understood here as the fulfilling of the commandments of God in such a way as to be admired and approved of by men. Again, Christ's comment is categorical: those who do this will receive their reward in this world, and from men: they can expect to receive nothing for their labours from God.

Finally, this Gospel tells us that there is a treasure, a reward, for which we can strive, but that it is not an earthly treasure, but one in heaven, "where neither moth nor rust doth corrupt, and where thieves do not break through and steal."

Where is this treasure of which Christ speaks? And what is this treasure? I would like to say something about this this morning. First, the place of this saying in the Gospel, the way it follows the previous saying in which Christ has been stressing the importance of the inner man, as opposed to the outer man, suggests that this treasure is not something outside of us, to be found in some "heaven above the clouds", but something within us.

Then, the combination of "treasure" and "hiddenness" reminds us of another saying, where Christ likens the Kingdom of heaven to a treasure "hid in a field, the which, when a man hath found, he hideth and for joy thereof goeth and selleth all that he hath, and buyeth the field." Here the treasure is the Spirit dwelling in each one of us, and the field, therefore, is ourselves. In order to take possession of the field, of ourselves, and therefore of the treasure, we must sell what we have, strip ourselves of all that ties us to this world, for otherwise the treasure of the Spirit, hidden within us, will never really be ours.

Finally, the image of a treasure, used so often by Christ to represent the richness of God's spiritual gifts to man, reminds us of the Parable of the Talents, where again worldly wealth is used as a metaphor for spiritual reality.

In the Parable of the Talents, God's initial gift of the Spirit is declared to be something that each one us can, by using it in the right way, increase. We can, in fact, according to this parable, lay up for ourselves treasures in heaven. We can, by following Christ's commandments, contrary to all human expectation, increase in ourselves the measure of God's grace. We can, to use the words of St Seraphim, "acquire the Holy Spirit."

So today's Gospel suggests that the period of Lent has as its goal our own personal growth through the forgiveness of others, through fasting and the struggle against hypocrisy. To these must be added, from the first part of Matthew 6 which was read at yesterday's Liturgy, prayer and giving of alms, and sharing of God's material blessings with others. All these things belong to the Great Fast and to our preparation for Pascha, for the celebration of Christ's Resurrection.

In all of them, Christ makes it clear that our goal is the acquisition of the Holy Spirit. Without the Spirit we cannot be true friends of God. Without the Spirit we cannot even begin to reverse the journey of Adam into exile, far from Paradise. Without the Spirit we cannot hope to enter into that intimacy with Christ which is the mark of his disciples. Without the Spirit we cannot hope to hear him call us friends. Amen.

21st February 1988

VESPERS OF FORGIVENESS

Now, at the beginning of the Great Fast, we turn our minds and hearts towards repentance, as the only true preparation for the celebration of Easter. It is the custom at this point to say a few words on this theme, and tonight I would like to do so by singling out and commenting on a verse from Scripture which occurs in the only service devoted exclusively to repentance, the service of confession.

Among the prayers we read in the service we find the words, "For thou, O Lord hast said (and the reference is to a passage in Ezekiel): I desire not the death of a sinner, but rather that he should turn from his wickedness and live." That is "I desire not the death of a sinner, but that he should *repent* and live."

God did not create man for sin, He did not create him for death, but that he should live a good and godly life as a companion and friend of God. And after the Fall, when man turned away from God, God, for his part, did not turn away from man. His desire followed him. And he still longs to have all men - to have *us* - as his companions and friends, that we should once again live with him, that we should once again "turn from our wickedness"- in the language of the Scriptures - "and live."

What is marvellous here is the way in which this turning, this repentance, becomes itself the source of life: life follows at once on repentance. Repentance leads to life. This is why the Great Lent, our preparation for Easter, can only be a time of repentance. There is no other preparation for sharing in the new life brought by Christ's Resurrection, than the turning which is repentance. Only that inner movement whereby we turn our backs on sin can prepare us for the joy that belongs to Easter. Without it our entry into that joy can only be superficial, psychological and external.

And yet how difficult it is to turn from death to life, to actually change direction! As in the material world for the direction of an object in motion to be changed, work has to be done. And no one of us can view this task with equanimity, for it involves being prised apart from our favourite entrenched positions, from recurrent and obsessive emotions, from the grip that certain situations, certain events - certain people, even - have on us. Only when we have been freed from these, have freed *ourselves* from them, can repentance really begin. Only then can we begin to turn our face towards God.

The first and most dramatic sign of our freedom from these "passions", as the Fathers call them, is the ability to forgive. Like love, forgiveness cannot be compelled. You cannot *make* anyone forgive you, you cannot even force *yourself* to forgive someone else. Love can only be given freely and forgiveness can only be given freely. And we will never have the freedom to forgive unless we first repent, unless we first, as preparation for repentance, free ourselves from the passions that bind our unrepentant souls.

As a sign that we have made a start on the path that leads through repentance to the joy of Easter, as an outward expression of the inward freedom which we all receive at the start of the Fast, we shall ask each other's forgiveness this evening. May this outward expression of our inner turning towards each other and towards God be a vehicle for us of God's grace, and a pledge of eternal life. Amen.

1 Cor. 8:8 - 9:2

What an extraordinary text is the passage from 1st Corinthians which we have heard this morning; extraordinary, that is, as part of our preparation for Lent. "Meat (that is, food) does not commend us to God: for neither, if we eat, are we the better; nor, if we do not eat, are we the worse." Today, when the fast in preparation for the paschal feast begins to bite for the first time, we are told, in a verse that is deliberately placed at the beginning of the pericope, that food does not matter when it comes to our relationship with God.

I do not want to take this opportunity to contradict St Paul and try to explain why it is that it is important that we should fast. This verse is read here on the assumption that fasting is the norm, an ordinary part of everyday Christian life, something that does not really need to be defended. And so these words have a special flavour to them in the Eastern Church, where fasting is bound up closely with the whole weekly and yearly cycle of liturgical prayer, and where fasting is simply accepted as one of the aids offered us by the Church tradition in our struggle to draw near to God.

In such a context, to say that food cannot bring us near to God is to say that when we have fasted, we have not yet begun. Its use here reminds us of the words of Christ to his disciples which are found in Luke 17:7-10: "Will any of you, who has a servant plowing or keeping sheep, say to him when he has come in from the field, 'Come at once and sit down at table'? Will he not rather say to him, 'Prepare supper for me, and gird yourself and serve me, till I eat and drink; and afterward you shall eat and drink'? Does he thank the servant because he did what was commanded? So you also, when you have done all that is commanded you, say, 'We are unworthy servants; we have only done what was our duty.'" Working in the field is nothing: it is expected. Yet in this passage from Luke there is a definite structure or sequence of events: first, the servants do the most ordinary things; then, they come in and serve their master directly: then, finally, they themselves sit down to eat.

So too with fasting. It is a most ordinary thing. No thanks are due us if we keep the fast. And yet, if undertaken properly, it becomes a preparation for our serving the Lord. Its meaning does not lie in itself, but in what it prepares us for, in what follows. It is serving the Lord that draws us near to God, not the fasting itself. And finally, it is this waiting upon the Lord, this service, that is the necessary preparation for our own sitting down to table, for our own entry into the realm of grace.

So let us accept St Paul's words in this light: fasting by itself will not commend us to God; more is required. Attention to the needs of others; to the needs of the community, the need to put what knowledge, what understanding we may have at the service of others, in whom is Christ. And finally, to take up the theme on which the passage from St Paul ends, we need to think in terms of apostleship. Fasting in the service of apostleship. To some degree we should all of us be able to say, as we look around us, "Are you not my work in the Lord? If I am not an apostle unto others, yet doubtless I am to you: for you are the seal of my apostleship in the Lord."

So let us not treat fasting as a "thing in itself", but relate it to other more important requirements of the Christian life. In this way we will find for it its true place in the economy of our existence, as a form of preparation for the service of God. Amen.

10th February 1991

SUNDAY OF ORTHODOXY

John 1:43-51

The passage which we heard this morning from the Gospel of John is one of several in which the Evangelist records incidents that show, in John's own words, that Jesus "needed not that any should testify of man: for he knew what was in man." And for this reason it is dear to me, as it is probably dear to all of us. The words which Jesus speaks in in response to Nathaniel's question: "Whence knowest thou me?" are a confirmation of our own deepest understanding - that we are known of God before we know Him; that, strange as this may seem, our lives are of greater interest to Him, than His is to us.

Placed as it is at the beginning of John's Gospel, this incident, together with Jesus' recognition by John the Baptist, His calling and naming of Simon Peter and the miracle of the wine in Cana of Galilee, serves as a second non-theological introduction to the Gospel as a whole: John wants us to know that with Christ something new has come into the world, a person capable of speaking to man with all the authority of God, and of changing him. In this context the miracle of Cana itself does not look forward to the Eucharist, but is a comment on the calling of the disciples, on the change that takes place in *them*, as they begin to shed the old man and put on the new man, being transformed

44

inwardly after the image of Christ, their master and guide.

In today's Gospel Jesus points to the source of His authority and power when He tells Nathaniel that he shall "see greater things than these," that "hereafter (he) shall see heaven opening and the angels of God ascending and descending on the Son of man." He speaks here of Himself, but alludes at the same time to Jacob, who once in a dream saw a ladder reaching from earth to heaven, and angels ascending and descending on it, linking the two, while God stood at the head of the ladder and spoke to him personally. When Jesus uses this image, then, He says that God is speaking personally to Him, and that His words are grounded in the words of the Father. As we read later in the Gospel: "Whatsoever I speak, therefore, even as the Father said unto me, so I speak."

But there is a difference between Jacob's vision and what Christ promises that Nathaniel shall see. In Genesis the ladder links heaven and earth; in the Gospel the angels ascend and descend upon the Son of man. And for us this difference is very important.

From the beginning of the world until the first coming of Christ, God dealt with the world solely as Creator. The world was his and he was active in it, guarding the people of Israel, illumining the prophets, giving wisdom and understanding to the the kings. But with the Incarnation God ceased to act only as Creator and began to be active as a creature as well. By becoming man, God began to work *within* the world he had created. And from the moment of the Incarnation, the whole of Creation has had a different relationship with God: it has become "God-bearing". Whereas at the beginning God "clothed himself with light (that is , with the divine energies) as it were with a garment", in these latter days, he has clothed himself with flesh, becoming man, emptying himself that he might finally fill all things from within.

And this is ultimately why we are able to celebrate the the veneration of icons today. Because every icon of Christ, or of his saints, no matter how inadequate it may be, is a reflection of the incarnation of God, it is a step, however tentative, in the direction of the End, towards God's being "all in all", towards the coming of the heavenly Jerusalem, that city whose light will shine from within. The holy icons also shine, however dimly to our eyes, with the light of God, reminding us of one who is "the light of the world", the life and light of man, the Son of God become the Son of man, "in whom dwells all the fulness of the godhead bodily."

May we too strive to realize in ourselves what the icons which we venerate proclaim: that God has become man in order to share with man his own eternal life. He has done this because he knows and loves us, and because he longs to see the angels of his glory descend and ascend upon us as well as upon his Son, Our Lord God and Saviour Jesus Christ. Amen.

11th March 1984

Reverend hierarchs, fathers, brothers and sisters in Christ!

I hardly need to remind you why we have met to celebrate Vespers together tonight: we are here to join in a common memorial of what has come to be called "The Triumph of Orthodoxy", the final, definitive restoration of the veneration of icons in the Byzantine Church by the Empress Theodora, acting for her young son, the Emperor Michael III, on 11th March 843. Today is 8th March, but that earlier day was also the first Sunday in Lent, and so, in terms of the Church's calendar, the two days coincide.

But our celebration this year is distinctive in its own way. This year, 1987, marks the 1200th anniversary of the 7th Ecumenical Council, held at Nicea in 787, and it was at this Council that the doctrinal basis for the veneration of icons was discussed and clarified. And it was the work of this Council which was finally, after great struggles, received, accepted, and ratified by the

47

whole Church on that first Sunday of Lent in 843, whose memory we keep this evening.

Now what is interesting about the 7th Ecumenical Council is that its decisions, and the theology they imply, were not only imperfectly understood by the Western Church - and therefore, in a sense, never truly received by it - but that the Eastern Church was content from that time on to live with icons, to integrate them completely into its liturgical life, into its prayer, yet never felt any need to develop its theological understanding of the icon as such. The Eastern Church was content to bring the art of icon painting to an extraordinary level of spiritual beauty and depth, while feeling no need to explain - to itself or to others - just what it was doing.

In a short anthology of texts concerning icons which was collected by Bishop Kallistos and published in 1976, there is not a single passage cited which belongs to the period between 869 and 1945! For over a thousand years the icon lived in Church surrounded by prayers and hymns, but also surrounded by theological silence. The painting of icons reached great heights - and depths - but it was in this century, the 20th century, that the icon was "reborn" as a concern in theology: the theology of the image, of the icon, was seen to offer telling insights into the relationship of God to man, and man to the world, insights which speak to contemporary people in their contemporary situation.

What I want to say tonight is that we - all of us - must come to terms with what the icon means, with what the image means, if we are to bear true and effective witness to God in the modern world.

What the 7th Ecumenical Council stressed, and what the Fathers have said, is that the icon, the true icon, is an opening - like a window, or better yet, a door - onto the hidden world of God, through which, in return, the grace of God is communicated to man. It is as if the icon is empty in itself, as if it has no purpose but to point beyond itself, as if it not a "thing in itself", but something open-ended. Open-ended in both directions, opening out in one direction towards God, and in the other direction towards ourselves and towards the world.

This is why Christ can be called the icon of God, the image of the Father; to see Him is to see the Father through him: "Who has seen me has seen the Father," as He himself has said: the image here is perfect, and through it the divine, personal source is visible.

This is why the saints are icons of Christ, images of Christ. To see the saint, to be in his presence, is to see Christ, to experience through him the presence of

Christ. The saint is in some sense empty: he - or she - is only a vehicle for the love of God towards us, and, in the other direction, a vehicle for our love towards God.

And this is why the images we have in church are icons: they too are not "things in themselves"; they, too, are in some sense empty; they, too, through their emptiness, put us in touch with the reality they depict, whether Christ, the Mother of God, or a saint. They, too, are vehicles, enabling us through them to offer the worship due to God alone and the veneration due to His saints, while at the same time enabling Christ, or the saints, to be present in our lives.

All this we know, all this we are aware of, whether consciously or unconsciously. But why do I say that we must keep all this in mind if we are to bear true witness as Christians in our present world? Because the world itself is in some sense an icon of God, an image of God related to the Father through the Son, through the Logos or the Word of God, who sums up in Himself all created forms, who is the focus, the meeting point, of the deep structure of all created things.

But man is also a creator. In his freedom he adds to what God has done, bringing to light new things. And man's creations can be either transparent or opaque. They can either be open, like icons, to the grace of God, to God's presence with us through His Son, or they can be closed to this presence, unable to let the light through because they are the distorted products of distorted human souls.

No doubt all that we do, all that we create, is touched at some point by the Fall. But the icon bears witness to the fact that there is a way back for man. That man is the creator, the maker of his world, that he is not condemned to an ever-increasing estrangement from God or to the creation of an ever more opaque world. There is a corner that can be turned. Man can create forms that help God to be present in this world, forms that do not shut Him out.

This has been true in every age. But today, when we are surrounded by so much ugliness of man's own making, we can be thankful that we have the icon to remind us of the final goal of all human activity: to so "image" God, that God can become present through us in the world. We can do this in our relationships with one another; we can do this also in the material forms and objects which we create. Our goal is the same: that in what we do and what we make, God's grace may find a home, may shine through.

In the words of the Gospel: "Ye are the light of the world... Let your light so shine before men, that they may see your good works, and glorify your Father which is heaven."

It is by becoming better images of God, better "icons", that we enable the light and grace of God to flow through us more freely. It is by following Christ's commandments that what we do in relationship to one another will lead others to glorify God. It is by creating icons in the material world that we render that world transparent to the grace of God.

Brothers and sisters, we need to take the theology of the icon from our churches out into the streets. We need to apply it to today's world. So much of what we see around us is opaque, dead, impervious to the grace of God. So much speaks not of God's glory, but of the fallen state of man. There is much that we can do, each in his or her own way. Let us begin with ourselves. Let us use this Lent to begin at least to restore, through God's grace, our own likeness to our Creator. But let us never forget that what we do - and what we make, what we design, what we create - can be open to God's grace. This is the message of the icon, and it is a message which we must take with us into the world. Amen.

8th March 1987

ST GREGORY PALAMAS

Mark 2:1-12

There is a connection, at a very deep level, between the two Gospel passages which were read today: the one for the Sunday, the story of the healing of the man sick of the palsy - that is paralyzed - and the passage from John 10:9-16 read in memory of St Gregory Palamas, in which Christ speaks of himself as "the good shepherd, who gives his life for the sheep." This link is to be found in the nature of forgiveness.

We know that our forgiveness by God is bound up with the story of the life, death and Resurrection of Christ: Forgiveness Sunday, at the beginning of Lent, anticipates Holy Week and Easter. At the Last Supper, Christ himself, in the very words which he speaks, draws the connection between his own death on the Cross and "the forgiveness of sins". But how does all this work? In what way does Christ's death show forth, and therefore effect, the forgiveness of *our* sins? And how does this relate to our own experience of forgiving and being forgiven?

The story of the healing of the man sick of the palsy is about the giving of life. Not that he was dead, but that he could not live fully: he had to be carried into Jesus' presence on a bed borne by four of his friends. By enabling him to walk, Jesus effectively gives him life, a fulness of life which he did not have before. But Jesus also forgives him his sins: "Son, thy sins be forgiven thee." And it is quite clear that we are intended to think of his bodily healing, his rising - itself an image of the Resurrection - and the forgiveness of his sins as interconnected. On one level because they are an element in Jesus' defeat of his immediate adversaries, but on another and deeper level because both are reflections of the love and power of God. Both are the gift of new life.

And it is at this point that Mark approaches the passage from John where Christ says that he has come to give life to his flock: "that they might have life, and that they might have it more abundantly." Here, however, the gift of life is associated with self-sacrifice, the gift of oneself: "I am the good shepherd: the good shepherd giveth his life for the sheep." To see the connection between these passages is to see how it is that God can forgive us through the death of Christ on the Cross.

To forgive someone - if we put aside all objective, juridical notions on the subject - is to give them new life. It is not simply an acceptance of them as they are, and an acceptance of whatever it is that they have done. It is an active blessing of their life. It is a turning outward: it is a gift of self. You cannot forgive and at the same time hold back. If you do, you will be forgiving only partially. If you keep anything for yourself at that moment of forgiveness, you have blocked the flow of life which is forgiveness.

And here we can see why God's forgiveness of man seems to require Christ's death on the Cross. Not because man's crimes merited death, so that Christ died for us in the sense that he accepted to die in our place, suffering vicariously for our sins. But because forgiveness itself, if it is to be full, complete, is by nature the giving of life that the death of sin may be overcome. To give one's life to the full is ultimately to die, and an immortal God could die only by becoming man for our sakes. It is Christ's death on the Cross that incarnates the forgiveness of God: the Good Shepherd giving his life for the sheep.

But if God must die in order to effect the forgiveness of man, surely *we* must somehow die if we are to forgive one another. And this is what we experience in practice: the reason it is so hard to forgive is that we find it difficult to die, to put aside even for a moment the concerns which we use to shore up our lives, and simply to live utterly, be it for a moment, for another.

This in spite of the fact that we know, again from experience, that to forgive someone is to open oneself out to the grace of God: it is to live, and to live more abundantly. Forgiveness which is more than abstract, which is a gift of life involving one's own death, which is an emptying of self, a gift of self, and leaves in us a grace-shaped hole which God is pleased to fill.

So let us, in the course of the Fast, try to realize in our own lives, in relation to one another, what Christ has given us on the Cross: Forgiveness. For just as Christ found life through death, so we, dying the death which is forgiveness, can also, by God's grace, enter into eternal life. Amen.

11th March 1990

This morning I wish to say just a few words about one feature of today's reading from the Gospel of St Mark - the healing of the man 'sick of the palsy', that is, suffering from some kind of paralysis. And what I wish to point out is something you have probably already noticed: that the healing in this story is not dependent upon the faith of the sick man only, but on that of his friends as well: "And when Jesus saw their faith, he said unto the sick of the palsy, Son, thy sins be forgiven thee." Forgiveness leads on to the healing of physical illness as well. If this account had ended as do other miracle narratives, we might expect to read, instead of "Go in peace, thy faith hath made thee whole," rather "Go in peace, the faith of thy friends hath made thee whole."

Now this passage is one of the most important in the Gospels for what it says about the Church, and about mankind in general. We are accustomed to rely upon St Paul to teach us about the Church, especially about the Church as a Body of Christ, a single organic whole in which each member, like the members of our own body, is distinct, unique, and contributes in its own particular way to the well-being of the body in its entirety; where each, ultimately, is necessary for the well-being of the whole.

But this is not just St Paul. This understanding of human relationships in the Church is also that of Christ, as is clear from the passages in St John where Christ speaks of Himself as the vine, and of His disciples as the branches. It is the same picture of organic unity that we find in St Paul, with the vine stock playing the integrating role in St John that the head plays in St Paul's language about the body of Christ.

What we have here is what I would like to call the "co-inherence" of human beings simply as individuals, as persons. This vision of human relationships, which is so different from that provided by the classical Greek and Roman world, and in particular by the Greek city-state, is characteristic of Hebrew, Jewish thought. Christ's own image of the vine goes right back to Psalm 80.8, where Israel as a whole is spoken of as a vine: "Thou hast brought a vine out of Egypt; thou hast cast out the heathen and planted it. Thou preparedst room before it, and didst cause it to take deep root, and it filled the land." So the Church, the New Israel, is understood in the same organic way as the Old Israel which God brought out of Egypt.

But there is a difference between them, and that difference is highlighted by today's passage from St Mark. The unity of the Old Israel, the co-inherence of the Old Testament "people of God", is in a sense rooted in nature, on a person's being one of the "children of Abraham", a descendant of the patriarchs. The unity of the New Israel, the Church, and the co-inherence of its members, is based on love. Somehow it transcends nature, and frees man from the constraints of nature. The life of the Church does not come from below, from the natural order alone, but also from above, from God.

This we can see from the Gospel narrative. It is not simply the faith of the four friends that makes it possible for the paralytic to be healed, but love, active love, a love which quite literally is willing to bear the burden of another, and to bring that other to God. It is love that holds together these five men so closely that the faith of all can be applied to one; which binds them so closely that Christ can treat their faith as if it were the faith of a single person.

This corporate understanding of the Church may not suit the individualistic attitude towards human relationships that is encouraged in society today. But it is the understanding of the Tradition, of the Apostles, and of Christ. And it explains, on the one hand, why we baptize children, and why Christ was able to heal the man sick of the palsy on the basis of the faith of his friends. It explains why, in the Epistle to the Hebrews, in a passage which we have all heard read many times, St Paul can speak of all the Old Testament righteous who preceded Christ and prepared the way for Him and His Church, and say: "And these all, having obtained a good report through faith, received not the promise: God having provided some better things for us, that they without us should not be made perfect" (Heb.11:39-40).

We are dependent upon each other, whether it be for healing or for our final resurrection in Christ. For the latter we can do little more than wait in hope - together; but for the former we can begin to work right now. We can begin to pray. We can begin to bear each other, to lift each other inwardly and carry each other on our shoulders until we have placed each other at the feet of the Lord. Surely, when He sees us do this, if only in our hearts, He will recognise this expression of our faith for what it is: an expression of our love, and will hear our prayer, the prayer of a body where each member co-inheres in every other.

Let us pray for each other, that our common faith, our common love, may make us whole. Amen.

10th March 1985

THE VENERATION OF THE CROSS

Mark 8:34 - 9:1

"There be some of them that stand here, which shall not taste of death, till they have seen the kingdom of God come with power."

Every year at this time we hear these words. Every year at this time they are proclaimed in church, and this great promise of our Lord is repeated. Why should this be so? Is it simply a historical statement? Is Christ just saying that, before some of those present at that time die, He will be raised from the dead and borne up to heaven in glory?

This cannot be true. The Gospels were written at a certain time in the past and for a particular audience; Christ's earthly ministry took place at a particular moment and He spoke to particular people. But Christ's words, and the words of the Gospels, are also addressed to us: they transcend the narrow limits of history and speak to us today. The promise we have heard today is addressed to us: there are some of *us* who will not die before we have seen "the kingdom of God come with power."

But what does it actually mean: "to see the kingdom of God come with power?" The Gospels do not tell us explicitly, but St Mark does clearly suggest an answer when he places his account of the Transfiguration immediately after this verse. The coming of the Kingdom of God is associated with the Transfiguration of the Son of God become the Son of man. In other words, it is associated with our transfiguration as well. When Christ says that some of those who hear Him will, before they die, experience, "see", the coming of the Kingdom, He is telling them that in their own lives they will experience the transforming, transfiguring power of God.

In Christ's own life this experience has four central "moments", points at which the process of transfiguration is most clearly revealed. First, at His baptism, when the Spirit descends upon Him. At that time, according to an early tradition of the Church not recorded in the Gospels, flames of fire broke out on the surface of Jordan. Then, at the Transfiguration itself, when Peter, James and John saw Christ's garments become white as snow, shining with the uncreated energies of God. Then, at the Resurrection, when through the power of the Holy Spirit the incarnate Lord crossed over bodily, as a man and as Man, into the world to come. And finally, at the Ascension, when Christ takes His place at the right hand of the Father. As both God and man He is, from that time, uncircumscribed.

But what about ourselves? How can we come to experience in our lives this coming of the Kingdom with power, this transfiguration to which we are called? To begin with, we have been baptized. Through the grace of the Spirit we have mystically died and risen again with Christ. We have received, in Chrismation, the gift of the Holy Spirit which the Apostles and disciples of Christ received at Pentecost. All this has been given us. The power of God is with us. And yet, have we seen the coming of the Kingdom in our lives? Have we known, through our own experience, what transfiguration can mean? And if not, why? What stands between us and our entry into our inheritance?

Brothers and sisters, what stands between us and our inheritance, between us and the Kingdom, is death, our own death. We have not died inwardly, and thus are unable to appropriate the gift of eternal life. In today's Gospel, just before He speaks of the coming of the Kingdom, Christ makes this clear, when He says that "whosoever will save his life shall lose it," while "whosoever shall lose his life for my sake and for the Gospel's sake shall save it." Somehow we must learn how to lose our lives, to surrender life as it is understood in the categories of this world, in order to inherit eternal life, in order to experience the coming of the Kingdom.

We must, in the end, become disciples of Christ, true disciples, learning from Him, hearing Him. We must come to understand what He means when He says: "Whosoever would come after me" - that is, whosoever longs to be where I am, who wishes to enter with me into the eternal Kingdom - "let him deny himself, and take up his cross, and follow me."

It is only by bearing all this in mind that we can see the force of the word "some" in the verse which I quoted at the beginning. It is not simply that some of those present at that time will die, while others will live to see the coming of the Kingdom. No. Most of those present would live out the year or two before the Crucifixion. But even of these, only *some* would see the Kingdom come with power: only those who would lose their lives, surrender them to God, only those who would take up the Cross of Christ, their cross, deny themselves, and follow Him. All others, even if still alive in the flesh, would not see the Kingdom, would not experience in their lives the power of God and transfiguration of man.

The promises of Christ are not the promises of men. The promises of God have all the force of physical law. They are built into the very nature of the world. Behind them is the same creative Word that brought all things from nothingness into being. When Christ says that some who stand here - here, today, in this church - will not taste of death, till they have seen the Kingdom of God come with power, these words are true, as true for us as they were for those to whom they were originally spoken. But those other words of Christ are just as true: "Whosoever will come after me" - whosoever wishes to be with me - "let him deny himself" and "whosoever shall lose his life" - lay down his life - "for my sake and the Gospel's, the same shall save it."

Let us use the Fast, and these few weeks that now remain before Easter, to make our own these words of Christ. The stakes are high: we can taste the sweetness of the Kingdom now, in this world, if we will die inwardly to this world. Or we can be among those who depart this life without ever having known eternal life, without ever having seen the coming of the Kingdom. Amen.

13th March 1988

ST JOHN CLIMACUS

Mark 9:17-31

The two Scripture readings we heard this morning - the passage from the Epistle to the Hebrews 6:13-20 and the passage from the Gospel of St Mark - have one important point in common: they both speak of Christ's death and Resurrection as a kind of journey. The Gospel does so by placing it in the context of Christ's going up to Jerusalem from Galilee, the Epistle more indirectly by speaking of Christ's passing through the veil to become a priest for ever after the order of Melchizedek.

In this Christ is the "Forerunner". He has travelled this path to Jerusalem. He has passsed through the veil of death into life before us and on our behalf. Our task in life is no more than to follow Him, to join Him where He is. And as we try to do so, we are not left behind alone. As Hebrews points out, Christ - even on the other side of death - is an anchor onto which we can hold, to which we are bound securely, by the cord of faith. He is our hope, our only hope; and this means that any hope we have in life which is not related to the Resurrection is not related to Christ, is not related to His victory over death.

Faith in God, faith in Christ, is bound up inextricably with hope. To have faith for a Christian is to have hope, to have hope for the Christian is to have faith. Jesus Himself makes the connection when He says to the father of the possessed child in today's Gospel, "If thou canst believe, all things are possible to him that believeth." In other words, even hope is possible for someone who believes, who has faith in God and in the power of God.

But what I want to say this morning is not particularly concerned with this, with the connection between faith and hope - at least not directly. I wish to point out first that our language about faith and hope tends to enshrine an error. We say, as if it were quite normal, that we have faith, that we have hope. I have been doing it myself. But there is a sense in which this is not true and cannot be true. Neither faith nor hope is a possession, a thing, an object, which we can hold on to, can cling to. In theological terms faith and hope do not belong to the realm of nature, but to the realm of personhood; they belong to the realm of freedom, not the realm of necessity.

And nothing could make this clearer than today's passage from the Gospel: "Lord, I believe; help thou mine unbelief." Here is a spiritual truth. The father, in tears, says what we all know, that faith and hope are not something we can hold on to, not something we can confidently possess. They are forms of relationship, they are bonds, and not what is bound. To use the image ofthe Epistle to the Hebrews, they are the rope that links us to the anchor, not the anchor itself.

Our language about love is much better in this respect. We do not normally speak about 'having' love, but about 'being in love'. And similarly it would be more accurate to speak of being *in* faith, of being *in* hope, when faith and hope are forms of relationships with someone else.

If we are truthful with ourselves we shall have to admit that we are not completely whole and stable in faith or hope or love. We can all of us add to the father's cry: "I hope, help thou my lack of hope," or "I love, help thou my lack of love." And yet today's Gospel tells us that Christ, in His mercy, can take our lack of faith and treat it as a fullness of faith. He can also take our lack of hope - or love - and treat it as fullness of hope or love. But only if we turn to Him with tears and confess both our lack and our longing for fullness and completion.

This is what it means for us to be on a journey: to have a destination and to know that we have not yet arrived, to anticipate the end and to know the distance that still separates us from our goal.

As we journey towards Holy Week and Easter, let us hold on in faith to the anchor of our soul - Jesus Christ, who has gone before and who draws us to Himself through death into the joy and fullness of eternal life. Amen.

24th March 1985

Today's Gospel is particularly appropriate for the fourth Sunday in Lent for three reasons: first, it contains one of Christ's predictions that He, the Son of man, will be delivered into the hands of men to be crucified and will rise again; secondly, it also contains, in the story of the healing of the young boy with a dumb spirit, a reference to the need for "prayer and fasting"; and thirdly, because at the very beginning of the passage Christ says to those around Him, to His disciples: "How long shall I be with you? How long shall I suffer you?" These words show clearly that Christ was pressing towards His Crucifixion; He was pressing towards it, pursuing it, as the final expression of the Father's will for Him.

It is in the context of this last feature of today's Gospel, which shows that Christ was in no way the passive victim of men's cruelty, but actively gave Himself for us, that I would like to look at another of Christ's sayings which we have just heard: "All things are possible to him that believeth." A "hard saying" if ever there was one. Is it true that all things are possible to someone who has faith? And if this is the case, do I have faith? These words stand as a challenge to our understanding and to our self-perception; to our minds and to our hearts.

What I want to suggest this morning is that "all things" has meaning only in relationship to Christ, and especially in relationship to His death and Resurrection.

We must realise for a start that Christ speaks here of Himself as well as of us. He speaks as the archetypal man, the archetypal human being in whom all that is human is contained, and in whom, before the end, the destiny of the human race is fulfilled. "All things are possible", when seen in relationship to Christ, means that resurrection is possible, that victory over death is possible; for death, as St Paul says, is "the last enemy". Only when death is conquered through resurrection will God be "all in all", only then will "all things have been fulfilled".

So "all things" in today's Gospel refers not just to anything, not to whatever we, in our fallen state, might think it would be nice to see. It refers specifically to our victory over death, in other words, to the fulness of God's will for us, not to the limitless profusion of our own desires. "All things are possible to him that believeth" means that for each one of us faith opens out onto eternity, onto victory over death in "little death" which we all already know from experience and face as well. Even Christ's command over nature, His walking on water or His stilling of the storm, has meaning only in the context of His Resurrection, as testimony to His victory over the power which the material world itself has of standing in the way of eternal life until transfigured and transformed by the power of God.

Here we reach a paradoxical situation, for "all things" that are possible for someone who has faith are compressed in practice into the framework of "thy will be done". The limitlessness of human potential, of human possibility, is constrained and limited by the uniqueness and the singularity of the will of God. Christ, the Lord of the universe, becomes in an instant the Christ of the Garden of Gethsemane, sweating drops of blood as He passes through the narrow gate that leads to eternal life.

Yet in a sense there is no constraint here; there is no constriction. For the cup that God asks Christ to drink contains all things. Everything that man could possibly desire in truth is offered to him through the Cross and Resurrection. The narrow gate that leads into the Kingdom is as wide as the universe itself - and wider, for through it has passed God. The prayer of Christ in Gethsemane, "Not my will, but thine, be done", contains all things for Him - and for us. It was the faith of Christ, the faithfulness of Christ, that made all things possible for Him, and brought Him through death to Resurrection.

All things are possible for us as well - but not outside the will of God. God's will for each one of us is that we should share, through faith, in Christ's victory; that when finally all things are subject to Christ, they should be subject to us as well, through our oneness with Him; that what has been give to Christ should be given to us as well.

Through the knowledge of Christ and His Cross, may we come to understand that "all things" are indeed possible for us through faith; and that this faith involves for us the acceptance of God's will, that narrow gate which opens out onto the Kingdom and eternal life. Amen.

9th April 1989

ST MARY OF EGYPT

Mark 10:32-45; Luke 7:36-50

This morning we heard read two passages from the Gospels: the first, from Mark, for the fifth Sunday in Lent; the second, from Luke, to honour the memory of Mary of Egypt, whose feast is transferred to this Sunday because her life is an "icon of repentance" and therefore suitable for our contemplation during Lent.

In any other year, I would have tried to preach on one of these two Gospels, which speak to us, on the one hand, of suffering willingly accepted and, on the other, of the need for repentance and forgiveness. But during this past week I was struck by one of the troparia read at the the celebration of the Presanctified Liturgy on Wednesday. This troparion refers back to the Parable of the Good Samaritan; it struck me because of what it says about the reasons why the priest and the Levite did not stop to help the man who had fallen among thieves.

The priest passed by, we learn, because he thought the man's wounds could not be healed; the Levite passed by "on the other side" because he was "unable to endure his soul-destroying agony".

Now the Christian life is a life of action. It is not just an ascetic struggle against temptation and against the weaknesses of our fallen nature, though this is essential. It is not just a struggle to purify our minds, our bodies, and our hearts, though without this we cannot hope to enter the Kingdom. It is a struggle to live as God lives, to share God's relationship with the world as far as this is possible for created beings. And this means being active. God does not sit back and look at the world. He is actively involved in the world. So *we* cannot sit back - cannot allow ourselves to sit back and look at the world. We are called by God, by Christ, to a life of incarnation in the world, and more specifically, to a life of active love.

But this itself is not without its relationship to the ascetic discipline of the fast. Part of the purpose of Lent is to help us see more clearly what it is that keeps us from sharing the life of God, from sharing his active compassion in the world. And two important obstacles to our doing so are given in the troparion that was read last Wednesday.

First, we don't really believe that these wounds can be healed. The problem is too great. Things have gone too far. Nothing can be done. If we look at ourselves, do we not find that we say this kind of thing all the time? We are constantly complaining, in effect, that the situation is hopeless, that nothing can be done. I have been reading recently a very interesting history of the Russian Church under Soviet rule, and what is clear from this

this book is that the Soviet government is constantly striving to convince the Church that "nothing can be done", that they - the Church - are powerless, that God is powerless. And what is also clear is that all that is good in the life of the Church is done by people who refuse to accept this point of view, by people who say, in effect, "these wounds can be healed". Something can be done. Not because we are powerful, but because God is powerful, able to act if we invite Him to act, if we open a way for Him by acting ourselves.

Secondly, however, we leave our stricken neighbour and pass by on the other side because we are unable, in the words of the troparion, "to endure his soul-destroying agony". In other words, because we are unable to enter into his life and make it our own, since this is too painful for ourselves. We are unable to go beyond an external "sympathy" and enter into the true depths of another person's life - because we are afraid, afraid of the pain, the vulnerability which this will bring.

And yet this is just what Christ has done. He has accepted to become so identified with us, to enter so completely into the frailty of our life, as to suffer with us our death. And He has done so with hope that should be our hope, the hope that in spite of the power of Satan, in spite of the rule of the Prince of this world, something can be done, not by man but by God, to overcome sin and destroy death.

The path He has shown us involves these two elements from the parable of the Samaritan: the belief that something can be done - "all things are possible to him that believeth" - and the deep identification with the suffering of another, the ability, the willingness, not to turn away because another person's suffering threatens to overwhelm us.

May our Lenten prayer and fasting help us to purify our hearts, so that we too, with Christ, may live in hope - and at the same time identify ourselves completely with the suffering and pain of those around us. Amen.

31st March 1988

The two Gospel passages we have heard today - the one for the Fifth Sunday of Lent about sacrifice, and the Gospel read for Mary of Egypt about forgiveness - are probably as dense a combination of texts as could be found. I can do no more this morning than point to some of the riches to be found in these passages.

What is the connection between sacrifices and forgiveness? What is the deep connection between these two texts which we are invited to look at in their relatedness this morning?

In the account of the woman who anointed Christ's feet and wiped them with her hair, we are told that the love which she shows in doing this is evidence of her forgiveness: evidence of her forgiveness by Christ, and ultimately - as only God can forgive sins - evidence of her forgiveness by God.

We are not told in the Gospel that this woman, who was a sinner, had repented of her sins: this is simply assumed - there is no forgiveness without repentance. But we are told Christ's last words to her: "Thy faith hath saved thee; go in peace." She has been reconciled to God: God's peace is with her; and the ultimate source of her repentance, which in turn has made possible the forgiveness of her sins, is her faith: her faith in a God who would receive her when she turned to Him. Faith in a God of love leads her to repentance, which in turn brings forgiveness; and forgiveness in turn engenders love. What is extraordinary is that all these come from God: faith, repentance, forgiveness, love: not one of these is something that we can do of ourselves, of our own will. We cannot say to ourselves: "Tomorrow I will have faith", the way we can say: "Tomorrow I will mow the lawn." Nor can we truly repent, simply by deciding to do so: we can change our external behaviour, but we cannot repent simply as an act of will. God's forgiveness and even our own forgiveness of our fellow human beings are not in our control.

And the love of which Christ speaks in today's Gospel, since it depends on prior forgiveness, is not something that we can just set out to do either. In all of this we are dependent upon the grace of God, upon God's mercy. Everyone who follows this path to peace will, to use the language of Christ, be "salted with fire". He or she will have been the recipient of God's grace at every stage. In him - or her - the fire of the Spirit will be at work to bring such a person to eternal life.

What of the other Gospel, then, which speaks of crucifixion and death, of the cup of sacrifice, of ministry, of a life given as a ransom for many and presented as a model for the disciples to follow?

In the same verse (Mk 9.49) in which Christ says that His followers "will be salted with fire", He goes on to say that "every sacrifice shall be salted with salt". In other words, on every sacrifice the Holy Spirit will descend. It will descend as fire descended from heaven to consume the offering made by Elijah on Mount Carmel (1 Kings 18:38), to set alight the young bullock which had been offered, together with the wood and stones and dust that had been soaked with water at Elijah's command.

What I want to suggest this morning is that the salting of the sacrifice, which must precede, according to Christ, the disciples' entering fully into the glory of their Lord, must be preceded in turn by repentance and forgiveness. The ministry of which Christ speaks must be preceded by reconciliation and atonement. It must be preceded by repentance and forgiveness: to imagine that we can enter into the ministry of Christ, become a servant as Christ became a servant, without first having reconciled ourselves to God - and to our fellow humans - through repentance is not possible. It is only through repentance that we can cease to seek lordship over others, as do the Gentiles, and freely accept to be least of all, the servant of all.

And this is why Mary of Egypt is commemorated on the last Sunday before Passion Week, the Sunday before Christ's Entry into Jerusalem and the beginning of his sacrifice: reconciliation with God through repentance is a prerequisite for true sacrifice, and Mary of Egypt in her flight into the desert is the supreme example of man's turning utterly and completely to God.

Our reconciliation with others may have to be one-sided. We may be able to do no more than repeat what Christ said on the Cross: "Father, forgive them; for they know not what they do." But a reconciliation must be there. It must be there if our sacrifice is to be salted with the Spirit, if it is to be a sacrifice that opens out onto eternal life.

As we draw near now to our celebration of the death and Resurrection of Christ, may we come to see repentance for what is it: the absolute essential for entry into the Kingdom. Amen.

27th March 1988

THE ENTRY INTO JERUSALEM

John 12:1-18

Today we truly enter Holy Week and no feast could make a better beginning for this week, which is the culminating point in God's plan for our salvation, than Palm Sunday, the feast of the Entry of Christ into Jerusalem. Not because of the element of triumph that is found throughout the services for the day (we shall come to that later), but because if we are to see what is really taking place on Good Friday, we must understand what is taking place on Palm Sunday as well.

There is a deep inner connection between the Entry into Jerusalem and the Crucifixion: one event illumines the other.

In neither do we actually celebrate the historical event, the event as it would be understood in the secular history of the world. This is quite clear in the case of the Crucifixion. We do not celebrate the death of someone who has become a nuisance to the civil authorities, whose presence has become an embarrassment to the religious authorities of Jerusalem. We remember the death of God, of the Son of God - something which these people did not see, could not see, something which, in their eyes, did not take place. But *we* see. In *our* eyes, the eyes of faith, it did take place; and we remember this event, this death, as something extremely precious to us, and to all men.

The same is true of the Entry into Jerusalem. We do not celebrate the triumphal progress of a messianic hero, we do not sing "Hosanna to the Son of David!" to a king who would wrest power from the Romans and restore it to God's people. And yet this is what the crowd was doing on that day. They shouted and cheered the Entry into Jerusalem of someone whom they thought would solve their problems for them - their political, social, cultural - even personal - problems; someone who would free their nation, would re-establish a theocratic, God-centred state. And the Gospels suggest that some at least of the disciples shared this understanding and joined their voices to the general acclaim.

Yet this is not what we celebrate today. As far as the Church is concerned, this messianic hero, as understood by the crowds, did not exist. Yes, we shout and sing: "Blessed is He that cometh in the name of the Lord," but our notion of what these words mean is quite different from that of the people who greeted Jesus on that first "Palm Sunday". They expected victory, visible, obvious victory; we expect suffering and death.

In Christ a reversal of values has taken place; even the meaning of words has changed. To "come in the name of the Lord" does not mean to come in triumph, surrounded by popular acclaim; it means to move quietly, silently, at that hidden point where the created world is changing its direction and returning to God. We can almost hear Christ say of the crowds, as he would say of his executioners a few days later, "Forgive them; for they know not what they do."

Christ does not exhort his followers, he does not encourage them as he moves before them to Jerusalem. The words of the crowd may cheer them, may give them courage; but Christ's words, his veiled allusions to his own suffering, leave them chilled and afraid. Not at this point could Peter say, "Lord, it is good to be here."

The meaning of what is taking place is ambiguous: a woman annoints Christ's feet with oil to honour him - and he says that she has done it for his burial. The disciples share the Passover with Christ as friends - and he links the blessings with his death. All is ambivalent. The tension between appearance and inner reality becomes acute, almost oppressive. Christ speaks confidently of his Second Coming, and all the while he seems to be headed for disaster, for destruction. Finally, disloyalty, meanness and treachery come to the surface among the disciples themselves. Nothing is as it seems. And in the midst of this Christ is seized, condemned and slain.

Yet through all this, Christ quietly remains what he was and is: "He that cometh in the name of the Lord." But the words now have new meaning. No longer can they refer to worldly triumph, to the victory of one man over another, no matter how worthy the cause. They can only refer to one who moves and lives at the point of calm, of quiet, because in him, and around him, the world, in its passion for destruction stops - and turns toward God.

It is with this knowledge, this understanding, with these eyes that we watch Christ today enter Jerusalem. And may we continue to watch him with those eyes through the coming week, until we see that the goal of his path, for him and for us, is resurrection in God. Amen.

11th April 1982

VESPERS OF GOOD FRIDAY

Christ our God is dead.

He did not die because He wanted to die, though He did so freely, willingly. He did so that He might bring salvation and eternal life to all men. And shortly before His death He prayed that He and we should be one, as He and His Father are one.

How often do we think that if we are to be one with Christ, we must be one with Him in His death, that we must die with Him?

Those who have already seen in their lives some part of the glory of Christ's Resurrection, who have caught even a fleeting glimpse of its radiance and beauty, are tempted to look only for this glory, and to judge their lives only by the extent to which they live in it.

Yet if we are to be truly one with Christ, we must accept to be one with Him in death. We must rejoice in it! We must thank God that we have been allowed to share with Him His cross, His descent into Hell. For it is out of death that Christ has won his victory; it is out of death that He has won for us eternal life!

Let us share His death, let us share His apparent defeat at the hands of the powers of this world, that out of death we may be one with Him in the joy of His Resurrection.

Christ our God is dead!

Glory to thee, O God; Glory to thee, O God; Glory to thee!

3rd May 1975

We have followed during this Holy Week the path taken by Christ; we have witnessed His entry into Jerusalem, His betrayal, crucifixion and death; and now we stand before his tomb. What can we say? What words can express our sorrow? We have approached the centre of the world, we have drawn near to our Creator only to find Him dead. Our God is dead. And yet that death is the gate, the only gate to eternal life. It is by dying that we are born, it is through death that we are renewed. It is by sharing in Christ's suffering that we prepare ourselves to share in His Resurrection.

Let us all draw near to venerate Christ's winding sheet. Let us come to greet our God. Never has God drawn so near to us as now, never is He so close to us as He is in death.

20th April 1979

We stand here this afternoon before the silent body of our Lord and Master, Jesus Christ, the incarnate Son and Word of God, who came forth from the silence of the Father to speak to us of love, and now lies before us in the silence of death.

How deep is the silence of God! And how it speaks to us! In it all meaning is contained: all righteousness, all judgement, all mercy, faith and love. No words can tell us more of God than can the silence of Christ's death.

As we come to venerate our Lord, let us enter the silence that contains his love, let us see in that silence the perfect revelation of God's love for us. Amen.

6th May 1983

GLOSSARY

Cheesefare: The last Sunday on which animal products may be eaten before Easter.

Chrismation: The second part of the Orthodox baptismal service. The baptised person is anointed on all parts of the body with a specially consecrated oil as the priest says, "The seal of the gift of the Holy Spirit." Only then will he be admitted to communion. It corresponds to Confirmation in the Western Tradition.

Great Fast: The Great Fast, or Great Lent, lasts for seven weeks before Easter, and is called "Great" to distinguish it from the lesser fasts. The fast before the Nativity of Christ (25th December) lasts forty days, before the Feast of the Dormition of the Mother of God (15th August), two weeks, while the fast before the Feast of St Peter and St Paul (29th June) varies in length depending on the date of Easter. For the Orthodox fasting means the abstention from all meat, fish, cheese, eggs, and other animal products. In the monasteries oil and wine are not taken as well. Wednesdays and Fridays are normally fast days throughout the year.

Meatfare: The last Sunday on which meat may be eaten before Easter. This falls one week before the beginning of Lent.

Presanctified Liturgy: Properly, the Liturgy of the Presanctified Gifts. The Orthodox Church fasts even from the Divine Liturgy on weekdays during the Great Lent, and therefore, to strengthen the faithful, a specially consecrated Lamb, or host, is reserved from the previous Sunday to be given in communion on Wednesdays and Fridays at the end of Vespers. The title of this book, *The Light of Christ*, is taken from the Presanctified Liturgy, during which at one point the priest blesses the congregation with a lighted candle, saying, "The light of Christ shines upon all."

Prosfora: A small loaf of bread which is available at the back of the church and is given to the priest by the parishioner with a list of names of those for whom he wishes the priest to pray.

St John Climacus (c.570-649): At the end of his life John Climacus (John of the Ladder) was abbot of the Monastery of St Catherine on Mount Sinai. He is remembered for his *Ladder of Paradise*, in which, in thirty chapters or "steps", he discusses the virtues and vices, and describes the path to dispassionateness, which is presented as an ideal of the Christian life.

St Mary of Egypt (5th century): The subject of a *Life* by Sophronius of Jerusalem which is read in church during the fifth week of Lent. She is said to have been a courtesan in Alexandria who, after joining a pilgrimage to Jerusalem and finding herself physically unable to cross the door of the Holy Sepulchre, was dramatically converted and spent the rest of her life atoning for her sins. See Sr. Benedicta Ward, *Harlots of the Desert'* (Mowbray 1987).

St Gregory Palamas (c.1296-1359): Archbishop of Thessalonika from 1347, he is known for his defence of the distinction between the essence of God, which is unknowable to man, and the energies of God, in which we can participate, experiencing them in the form of deifying grace.

Triodion: The Lenten service book of the Orthodox Church. A partial English version has been published as *The Lenten Triodion,* translated from the original Greek by Mother Mary and Archimandrite Kallistos Ware (Faber and Faber, 1978).

Troparion: A hymn verse honouring a a saint or feast, or commenting on the meaning of a particular event or biblical text.

Vigil Service : In the Russian parish tradition Vespers and Matins are combined and celebrated in the evening before Sundays and great feasts. It is in effect a shortened form of the All-night Vigil kept in the monasteries.

BIOGRAPHICAL NOTE

Father Basil Osborne was born in Egypt in 1938 but was raised and educated in the United States, where he became a member of the Orthodox Church. He holds a doctorate in Classics from the University of Cincinnati and has been Rector of the Russian Orthodox parish in Oxford since 1973. Since 1980 he has edited the diocesan quarterly *Sourozh. A Journal of Orthodox Life and Thought.* He is a widower, with three children aged 15-21 years.